HOLY WILD

HOLY WILD

GWEN BENAWAY

BOOK*HUG 2018

FIRST EDITION

 Canada Council **Conseil des Arts** Funded by the Government of Canada   Financé par le gouvernement du Canada    Canada
for the Arts **du Canada**

ONTARIO ARTS COUNCIL
CONSEIL DES ARTS DE L'ONTARIO
an Ontario government agency
un organisme du gouvernement de l'Ontario

The production of this book was made possible through the generous assistance of the Canada Council for the Arts and the Ontario Arts Council. Book*hug also acknowledges the support of the Government of Canada through the Canada Book Fund and the Government of Ontario through the Ontario Book Publishing Tax Credit and the Ontario Book Fund.

Book*hug acknowledges the land on which it operates. For thousands of years it has been the traditional land of the Huron-Wendat, the Seneca, and most recently, the Mississaugas of the Credit River. Today, this meeting place is still the home to many Indigenous people from across Turtle Island, and we are grateful to have the opportunity to work on this land.

Library and Archives Canada Cataloguing in Publication
Benaway, Gwen, author
   Holy wild / Gwen Benaway.

Poems.
Issued in print and electronic formats.
Text in English and Anishinaabemowin (Ojibwe)
ISBN 978-1-77166-439-4 (softcover)
ISBN 978-1-77166-440-0 (HTML)
ISBN 978-1-77166-441-7 (PDF)
ISBN 978-1-77166-442-4 (Kindle)

   I. Title.

PS8603.E5561H65 2018   C811'.6   C2018-904123-4
                                       C2018-904124-2

cover image by Quill Christie Peters
author photograph by Jon Elliot

PRINTED IN CANADA

... come celebrate
with me that everyday
something has tried to kill me
and has failed.

—Lucille Clifton, "won't you celebrate with me"

for all the girls like me

CONTENTS

PREFACE, BY QUILL CHRISTIE-PETERS • 11
AUTHOR'S NOTE • 15

Akii • 17
Girls Like Me• 20
White Passing • 25
Curiosities • 27
Transition • 30
Boys • 32
Endings • 34
Root • 36
Burrs • 38
Boys • 41
Dysphoria • 46
Heterosexuality• 51
Holy Wild • 55
Boys • 57
Reverberation • 67
Pretty • 69
Phoenix • 71
Forgiveness • 73
Olympia, Washington • 78
Fuck Your Fear • 85
A Love Letter For Trans Girls • 101
NDN Transsexual • 110
Niibii • 117
Tonight • 132

PREFACE: KWEWAG LOVE
THEMSELVES DESPITE ALL ODDS

QUILL CHRISTIE-PETERS

The air is still and humid with a slight warm breeze, the sheets of my bed crumpled against slightly damp skin. I am trying to relax so I can touch myself but sometimes it is so hard to relax when that space of slowness and deliberation allows you to see the parts of yourself that are broken. The ancestors call us back to our bodies no matter how far we travel from skin that feels hated and unworthy. The ancestors call us back to our bodies so they can sing them back into feeling loved and whole, flesh and stardust, earth and blood. Every time I touch myself, my body breaks open and from this rupture a steady stream of water from my homelands flows out onto the bedroom floor, sturgeon sputtering out onto the bed before vanishing, ancestors chuckling deep into their bellies. Drumming. Feasting. Touching myself under the moonlight.

The painting on the cover of this collection is entitled *Self-Portrait: Kwe loves herself despite all odds.* It is one of three paintings in the Kwe Series that explore my personal journey of self-pleasure, masturbation, and nationhood as a cis-gendered, heterosexual Anishinaabekwe grappling with the realities of gendered colonial violence within my body, homelands, and community. All three paintings are self-portraits that visually represent this specific brown body of mine that is shaped through my experiences of the world. And yet my body is so much more. These works seek to challenge the colonial compartmentalization of the body as limited to physicality by honouring my body as an indefinable ebb and flow of homeland, ancestors and spirit kin. My body cannot be compartmentalized from the places of creation I come from, and practices of self-pleasure are a profound and necessary resistance to the colonial project.

When I first read Gwen's work, I was deeply moved by her ability to articulate body, homeland, ancestors, and trauma in a way that spoke to my own understanding of who I am and where I come from. Although our respective work is solely embedded in our own experiences, we have found solace in each other's abilities to resist the compartmentalizations that reinforce colonial boundaries and to create sovereign space for Anishinaabekwe relationships to our bodies, our territories, and our communities. Gwen, brave and generous Anishinaabekwe, has invited me into her relationship with the world through beautiful words that weave homeland into body, ancestors into flesh. Likewise, I have invited Gwen into my own relationship with the world through images of the body as a site of diverse creation. We Anishinaabekwewag always doing the good work, the hard work, the work that gets us in trouble, the work that requires us to pause amidst the chaos to whisper to each other, *I see you, I love you, you move me.*

Exploring the relationship I have to my body is challenging and painful within a settler colonial project that continues to organize itself through the violence of cis-heteropatriarchy. I conceptualize these paintings of my body as gifts from my ancestors that help me feel worthy of feeling pleasure and wholeness and that help me love myself, my body, and where I come from. Now I gift this image of my body, this image of my interpretation of our greatest Anishinaabeg technology, to Gwen, Anishinaabekwe kin who has given me countless gifts through her words and presence. The gifting of this image is rooted in my relationship to Gwen, a sovereign act of mutual recognition that honours the ways we have found connection and collaboration through our work. I hope this image acts as a portal, an invitation, and as protocol from which to enter this beautiful collection of poetry. This protocol foregrounds Anishinaabekwewag sovereignty over our bodies, our homelands, and our relationships to one another and situates the agency and boundless love our ancestors and spirit kin have for us as the keepers of this Anishinaabekwewag space of sovereignty.

And then I am left lying on the damp bed and my skin feels like the softly rippling lake that is just beyond my window. The drumming softly shifts into heartbeat, the chatter of busy ancestors slowly fades into the stillness of a hot night. They will always whisper, calling me back to my body, guiding my hands to love and feel loved, dancing at the edge of skin that we are stars and sun and prayers and laughter, earth and blood and spruce and smoke.

QUILL CHRISTIE-PETERS is an Anishinaabe visual artist and arts programmer from Treaty 3 currently residing in Thunder Bay. She creates paintings that visualize the love our ancestors have for our bodies, our communities, and our homelands. Check her work at quillviolet.com and her insta at @raunchykwe.

AUTHOR'S NOTE

I use Anishinaabemowin (Ojibwe) words and phrases throughout this text. Anishinaabemowin is not a standardized language with a wide range of regional and community-specific variations in meaning, spelling, and pronunciation. As a second-language learner of Anishinaabemowin, my version incorporates several regional and community variations. I learned from fluent speakers and elders from across Anishinaabe territory and my language reflects that diversity. I relied on my memory of Anishinaabe words and what I was taught by my elders to translate my use of them in this text. My translations may differ in meaning from those of other speakers and may contain grammatical errors. My intention is to use Anishinaabemowin to speak to meanings that English does not contain and to reflect the richness of Anishinaabemowin as our first carrier of culture, knowledge, and worldview. I am not a fluent speaker, but I believe it is a responsibility and a gift to use our languages whenever we can, regardless of our fluency.

Akii[1]

ohmamaaminaan
mother of us all

give me the land,
call us by our name

she lives in marrow,
along the inner line

of shoreline I carry
⠀⠀⠀⠀⠀in the eye's inseam.

let me be hers,
daughter of everything

lakes and spruce, the mountains
under blackness.

⠀⠀⠀⠀*odakiimi*
⠀⠀⠀⠀*she becomes the land*

say I belong here,
this place, now—

for every time
they misgender me

by the wrong pronouns
the old name,

---

1 the land/earth

answer for me, Akii

gaawiin, nidanis

no, my daughter
is the same woman

I made her
at birth.

Akii, the land births us
apane[2]

infinite expansion
from wazhashk's[3] hand

becomes

a whole world, sudden birth
of a universe in water and mud

wayeshkad,[4] we were holy
now trannies are a white disease

still we return in rivers
grow in lakes

Akii is nimama[5] miinwa
Niibii is nimama

---

2 forever, eternally
3 muskrat's
4 long ago, in the past
5 my mother

two mothers make
      one daughter

cis ppl can do whatever
      they want to us

         murder the new life
shame the transformed

but we are apane kwe[6]
      we are Akii

nothing takes her from us
      and this is what makes us holy

even if we are the only ones
      who know it.

---

6   woman

Girls Like Me

I.

I want to walk in a lace dress
by a lake in autumn

silver on my neck, someone's hand in mine
wrapped up in the complications

of this willow heart and imperfect body.
I know love is a lie sold by the white

capitalist machinery, patriarchy, and Ikea,
my ancestors married for a season or two

with multiple lovers in every hunting ground
but it's a dream I've carried since

I can remember, why I transitioned
I couldn't imagine walking by a lake

as anything but a woman in a lace dress.
every part of it is stupid and small

how I want to feel the weight of baby
on my bladder, kicking up a storm

while I shuffle around swollen like a pear
in fleece pyjamas, calling my mother

to complain about humidity and cramps,

none of it will come as I want it,
the lake empty, my dress political—

I don't want to be a gender statement—
no mother to call, no family, no uterus

still this dream is as persistent as the grief it creates,
it lives on even if I can't imagine anything anymore.

2.

the most romantic thing you could say to a girl
like me, if you spoke to a girl like me at all,

would be

> *I noticed you right away*
> *everything you said felt*
>
> *like snow beneath my tongue.*

I know the most romantic thing boys say to girls like me,
if they say anything to girls like me at all,

is

> *you almost look like a real woman,*
> *for a second I thought*
> *you were worth something*
>
> *you can suck my dick if you want to,*
> *I've always wondered what it would be like*
> *to be with a girl*

like you.

I'd say what every girl like me says,
if we say anything at all, the most romantic thing
I can say

is

       for a moment I almost thought
          you were the boy
        I've been looking for

but you can stay
          until he gets here which

      will be never so

you can stay as long
as your curiosity keeps you,

               don't mind the snow

     it's what happens when the possibility
     goes out of water.

4.

girls like me get no easy breaks,
see us walking alone at 3 am

in shoes that hurt, in bodies that break
down streets we know

            can't be safe.

yeah we're the girls who sat in the back
with bottles thrown at our heads

a joke for everyone
        our voices a punchline

we're a public service ad for teen suicide.

girls who don't shut up when we really should,
our noses broken and our lips split,

heads caved in and wrists bent,
never too good for the second blow.

the fat girls, the skinny girls
                we're always hungry

learned how to hide and blocked our doors
with bed sets, hung ourselves with sheets and scarves,
        marks on our thighs.

queens and whores, the fuck-ups who are
never fucked, girls with laughs

        like runaway trains,

                    noise and fury

with nowhere to go, our bodies burning.

girls like me got it bad,
boy crazy even if

they call us sweet
        we make good friends
second mothers, confidantes

the trial sample, tester strip for sex.

throw us away, disposable girls

walking alone in an endless line
of bad ends, tough lessons.

        we're not the girls
they want but girls like me

                got our own medicine

they call us brave. we're just desperate
for a tomorrow that never comes,

yeah we're nothing if we're

            anything at all.

WHITE PASSING

I heard stories
of folks with Clorox, scrub the brown
      off their bodies

avoid the sun, pretend to be Italian
go to church, speak English.

I always thought those stories
sounded fake

couldn't imagine tricking
whites into ignoring
      our half-breed hearts.

then my transition,
      try to be a "girl"

listen to co-workers
      find my female voice
shave my legs twice a day

pluck every hair, pad my bras
grow my hair, wear pink

mimic women on the street
      date a straight guy.

try to pass
blend in

erase myself

full-time woman, 24/7
        tuck my dick even if it hurts
don't eat
because girls
        must be small.

now I understand
my elders' stories

how violence made me change.
if the only happiness we see
        in the world is them

        if the only escape
           is to disappear
    into them

whichever them it is
        whites or girls

we do anything we need to
even if we have to
        kill ourselves first.

CURIOSITIES

I.

I buy a dress for this maybe date
at a second-hand shop last Saturday, pink chiffon

smells of old perfume embroidered in black flowers

for our second date which may not happen
or may not be a date,

I can never tell who finds my body
desirable or curious,

I ask a boy if it's ok for me to wear a dress

> *will he be seen in public*
> *with a girl like me*

it feels polite to let him decide
if he is brave enough

> girls have to be sweet
> or we're worthless

he tells me to wear whatever feels pretty
as if I could feel pretty or if being a woman

was being beautiful, like pretty is something
I have access to in this body.

men shout faggot at me
wherever I go, threaten my body,

a woman spit at me today, her eyes
a disgust I can't unsee.

the dress hangs in my closet,
            untouched and soft

a dream of a life in a body I can't have.

girls like me can't feel anything like pretty,
the same way my grandmothers felt

when they were taught being Indian wasn't a crime
as long as you try hard

            to make your body disappear

it's only ok to be a tranny or an Indian
if you try to act like

            something else.

2.

museums for Indians full of our dead junk,
masks on walls, cut-up lodge poles,

the shells we threw away
sleep beside artifacts they stole.

they dug up our burials out near Peterborough
so deep the graves showed the skeletons

of dead kin, white eyes pour over the bones
like bleach across the remains of our humanity.

I used to think the worst was us

                    as school lessons

to be consumed, real only by their imagination alone.

after my transition, museums aren't so bad,
the glass cases protect the dead

                        from interrogation

but I can be touched
an NDN transsexual

walk through white people staring.

I think how easy it is to be a skeleton,
                  underground in a lodge

laid out and frozen, my heart still
safe forever from them,

if desecration is our destiny,

                let it come when I've gone
                to a place the living can't see.

Transition

no room for Indians, she told us
      76 years old

but we could still hear the wound in her throat
refuse to close, even if she knows it was wrong
of them to turn her away, that hotel in Kenora,
40 years ago or more, her sister and newborn
out in the snow, late night stumbling out to find

somewhere safe in a land that used to be ours

now, my small body in dresses and heels,
past men on the street, leers, catcalls, and laughs
charting safe pathways across the city, learning
to judge when someone's not safe, avoiding questions,
trying to make space for this body, its confused state,

the middle ground of gender is a killing field.

I know exactly what she meant when she said
we wanted to stay for a night before heading home.
they turned us away as if we were nothing at all
we cried but there was nothing to do but go on
say a prayer for people who hold such hatred

it must be worse to carry all that anger

than walk two miles through winter
to a bus station and wait all night
for a rescue you aren't sure

will ever come and yes, I know how she felt
but I can't say I have prayers

for anyone but myself.

Boys

mythic boys, every story is their home,
every mouth their temple,

their bodies fill the horizon.

without thinking, they
take all the air out of every room—

they're infinite.

I never wanted to be one,
never felt the magic of male freedom

on my skin, always afraid,

I used to watch the boys in flight,
as if I could learn to mimic their wings,

gain their power by osmosis.

is that why I fuck them?
is that why I love them?

not because they deserve it,

they don't, even if they're
magnificent beasts, but because

I want to swallow their souls,

wear their bodies over my femininity,
be as powerful as they are,

for a moment, know what it means

to fear nothing
but yourself.

Endings

on starting hormones and ending
a life that was never mine.

goodbye to cigarettes, the first five-second inhale,
excuses to be separate, outside the party, burning.

goodbye to Meg Ryan, Sandra Bullock, Sleepless
in Toronto, no more fever love dreams.

goodbye to invisibility, midnight walks along
streets of happy houses, spilling light and voices.

goodbye to easy answers, to a sacred private self,
wearing a dress without a revolution.

goodbye to the children I can't have,
no holiday plans with in-laws.

goodbye to the world I thought I wanted,

life in snapshots of longing, amber-tinted.
goodbye to everything that used to sing,

it isn't as hard as it seems, goodbye to stupid hope,
half-baked fantasies of a self I can't possess,

a woman I won't be.

goodbye to her dreaming, deep in the heart
of the universe, seed her bones with fire.

goodbye to desire's ghosts, the faces in smoke
of loves I will never see.

Root

if I had words for this change, they would be solitary lights
in a spring night by the pond,
       small, caught in frost and fog
       in the early hours of predawn,
the time my kookum[7] used to say
was when the dead
       come home.

I would line up the words like waterlogged trees
along the sunken bank, roots slipping into places
my eyes can't see, heart of an underwater forest
growing in the absence
       of warmth.

what sleeps in language is what sleeps in me,
possibilities and consequences
              for which the surface has no hope,
an unwritten alphabet of shadows
I learn in secret, undercover from a hormonal moon
in a dark tongue.

what I mean is everything is
       as far away as time,

what I mean is I don't recognize myself,
       an unspoken sound in a damp mouth

---

7 grandmother

in a snake tunnel along the shoreline of a life
          I can't describe.

what I mean is I don't mean anything more or less
than a slow tumble into waters
uncharted by anyone I know,

what I mean is a transition is as simple as pulling bark
from a tree without stripping
          what keeps it alive.

Burrs

1.

nothing to you, jumping over fences
to break the skin of a graveyard by night

under a full moon in a jean jacket.

you are a boy born to conquer every gentle place
in every woman you meet, always bent toward discovery

      a brave word your ancestors used

to disguise
conquest.

2.

chorus of night cars and mosquito bites
as dead bodies rot beneath us.

I brought you here to offer us to wonder—
your song to night, soft under stars.

when I touch you, I feel the weight of your love
like stones, a haunting in the eyes.

I wrap your ghosts inside my arms
as your hand traces my sternum.

when we move through the cemetery
I want to ask if you notice

the shadow
walking over graves

is you,
holding my hand.

3.

a moment, my hands above your face,

I pick burrs from your hairline,
say nothing, my eyes lock

to the horizon, careful not
to show you the soft light

in my eyes, I remember
                    the pain in my body,

heat along my fingers where our skin meets.

what do I say to a boy who thinks it's possible
for a girl like me to be anything more

than the inward curve
                    of a blackbird's wing,

always beating against desire.

I love you here, soft underneath me
unafraid by starlight

                    but I won't surrender

this want of you for anyone, even death.

maybe I ask more than we can give,
but tonight I want to be

        this shadow across your face
        more than any other light

I can be.

Boys

1.

the first time a boy kissed me,

I was as new as a snapped branch,
green in the spine.

every boy since, more than I remember
I was cold, mirrored their mouths

                in rough mechanics of instinct.

now my second body, a woman in bud,
everything is new,

this change gives too much light.

the next time a boy kisses me
I will crack open like new earth in rain,
soft as mud.

he'll taste spring,
                the whisper of snow.

2.

say you love contradictions,
place a hand between my thighs,

feel the soft small line of me,
transsexual clit is a boy cock

           gone over to water.

my breasts are smaller
than those of the girl you often fuck,

what I lack in volume,
          I make up in novelty.

hold me down with your body in me,
I'll be a river running west,

         my hips, a lake
           beneath you.

you like girls like me, it's ok
to want a body unfinished,

in (trans)it.

I'm more or less a woman,
you can be a boy as wide as sky,

cross borders, break boundaries inside me,
unlock us in a touch, bridge currents

before I become an ocean.

my cunt is a gift, your cock
a promise,

not a perfect love, our secret want
your tongue, my bones.

our hands still spark together—
we make new countries

where desire and our fear
bring us.

3.

every day I fought you
cut words like pine needles in your skin.

made visible a body you deny
called down fire from mishomisinaak[8]

wore a bruise in my skin
spoke tongues of grace and rage

shaped silence and emptiness
created beauty from nothing.

the record of my resistance
is a wound I carry in bone

still I lost you, this rough end
of your texts blinking at 3 am

my price is too high
you got more for less

                                          from cis girls

.

---

8 · the grandfathers/ancestors

no-cost easy love, no-consequence sex
my body costs your masculinity

still I claw back, reply as if
anything I say could hurt you

       the way you killed me.

still I would give everything up—

the early rain last Saturday
new shoots in the dog park

every white fleck of ash on my balcony

for a second chance to believe in today
          your hands across the café tabletop

move to mine but stop halfway
you aren't brave enough

         to touch me.

I wanna be new in your eyes
how I was our first time, under the weight
         of your chest

a different night where I'm not second best
a whole girl, not the monster I am now.

I want faith to pray as if
I could be the same

as every other girl
if only in your eyes

but nothing I have to give
is worth

        what she is.

DYSPHORIA

I.

write your heart in pieces,
cut the borders of what you hope.

you will not survive,
no matter how you sing,
            never mind prayers to fire
                      or dreams of river water.

surrender to doubt,
open to unravelling,

bend into the grace of loss,
be the bird in the house,
                the omen of change.

the girl who dies in every
                      wingbeat.

2.

the light never finds me.
                no miracles miinwaa

          ningwiinawenimaa.[9]

three months on HRT, my body swells.
        breasts bud upward   hips open like flowers.

---

9 I miss him

still nothing changes,
        I let a boy fuck me

to feel his hands on my skin,
        his cock

a hard pain in me, as if my softness
deserved a rough end,

as if I'm a good girl to take from behind
        then throw away.

no regret, no excuse,
I didn't cry out or ask

        him to stop.
        I want to know I am still real.

I want to be wanted, to have a body worth fucking,

        a body as giving as any other girl,

he's not the right boy and I'm not the right girl.
        ningwiinawenimaa apane

what's the point of rebirth if loss roots deeper,
        what I want is not what I hope for.

what I hope for is a love worth becoming

        but what I want is any love
                that's possible.

3.

my chances dissolve like ice floes on the river.
            nibabaamaadagaak[10]

everyone is already found,
            I'm the only girl left.

I watch them cross streets,
            move like sparrows home,

trail voices across the city to corner stores at 4 am,

I waited too long to be so I can give her nothing
she wants or needs,

            just loss and hormones.

a new life in an old death is a different way to lose.
now she's a pariah,
                        half a girl.

there's no excuse,
a girl waits soft in me.

I can't save her before
            fire makes her
ashes and embers,

a last whisper of light
before the dark comes
                        to wipe us clean.

---

10   I go about on the ice

4.

six months late, I start the pills to begin again
in another self, more myself and less me,

a mason jar filled with water and earth,
mud in veins,

a girl breaks open in me.

a soft change, invisible to light
felt in every step, and deep sleep

infinite exhaustion
             waits with me.

secret heart, burn and smoke.
dark in winter, a woman begins.

                nidaanji-bimaadiz[II]

underground in bones
             only she can touch.

5.

it doesn't matter what I or don't do,
photograph myself in dim light,

a girl hunts the boy to cut him loose.

[II] I change my life

the woman I am is bound in roots
of her longing,

becoming isn't easy.

I say this pain will pass,
what I mean
            is nothing changes,

even my breasts swell at night,
recede at dawn to nest in my bra,

they don't sing and promise doesn't bud.

my friends say hold on,
            soon I'll be washed out in hormone's moon tide,
                    my face dissolves.

but it doesn't matter what I do or don't do,
no one watches the edge of my life.

the only one here is me and what
I want is not what I hope for.

so I pray at night, worship wonder to cultivate
a worn love of being transsexual.

become the girl who vanishes
            the more she is seen.

HETEROSEXUALITY

Queer is a word someone invented to hurt
                then it was reclaimed, rebirthed.

I don't fit inside this history
                rainbow flags don't make me feel safe.

I've always pretended faith while denying my resistance.

what does it mean to be abandoned by the only people
                I've been allowed to call mine?

I'm caught in a new body with different boys,
                learning heterosexuality through bad nights.

they break my heart's hymen until I bleed forgiveness.

I keep going on dates with a straight boy.
                I don't know how to be this girl.

I text another boy between our dates
                who doesn't want to fuck me but wants my intimacy.

do boys deny my wholeness or do they deny their own?

on our first date, the straight boy says I look great
                his eyes on my breasts, embarrassed.

I can't imagine us fucking but we do.

I like him but I'm play-acting. I don't know my lines.
our second date ends in a subway corridor. he kisses me goodbye.

I don't say yes or no. does being a woman mean surrender?

do I want to be kissed by a straight man?
        he tastes like an apology.

my therapist asks my sexual identity so I describe my partners.
        am I who I let fuck me? or who I want to fuck me?

the other boy asks if him fucking me to validates me as a girl.
        he doesn't apologize for this so he erases me twice.

I am so afraid he's right though I know he isn't.

my gender isn't yours to deny or affirm (but I let you anyway).
        my desire is more than identity politics (but I feel nothing).

I have spent my life making space for male desire.
        giving comfort and absolution like a sexless mother.

I want a partner who isn't ashamed.

I give a softness that is not returned.
        I can't explain my body. fuck me or don't.

every time they deny me, I become more whole.
        every time they're scared to fuck me, I'm less afraid.

I don't hang with boys anymore. they want one thing but I'm many.

I text my friend "am I straight now?" she says "obvsly."
        the obvious thing about heterosexuality is no one is happy inside it.

the boys who fuck me are the only boys brave enough
        to embrace the soft and hard of themselves.

the other boy says he's my friend but caresses my breasts.

we lie beside each other, his fingers in my hair,
        his half erection outlined, my breasts swollen.

he asks if he's transphobic for how he treats me
        so I say yes but think "maybe I'm just not a real girl."

I blame him for everything but I'm just as fucked up.

sometimes I replay this moment and choose different paths.
        every choice we make ends in rupture.

cis boy + trans girl = nothing.

he calls me a week after fucking me
        to say he has no space for us,

I say he didn't do anything wrong
        but everything in me breaks.

I cry on the phone. I don't tell my friends about this part.

I keep texting him. it won't be violence anymore if we're friends, right?
        he likes my Instagram posts about trans desirability. is he saying sorry?

I go on a third date with the straight boy. he holds me while everyone stares.

he says he doesn't care what anyone thinks so I kiss him.
        he describes me to his friends and says *she* without any doubt.

he walks me home even though he's five stops away from his home.
        I am not used to the compassion of men nor their mercy.

the other boy says the straight boy not caring I'm trans is a warning sign.

when the straight boy breaks up with me, I think it's prophecy.
    he says he's not emotionally available. he didn't expect to feel this way.

he goes out of his way to explain it's not because I'm trans.
    all I think of is what the other boy will say if he finds out.

I've only been a girl for a year but I'm already bruised by boys.

    being a straight girl is living inside a violence you can't name.
    I delete my online dating profiles. I take a vow of celibacy.

what I want from boys is not queer or straight, feminine or masculine,
    but fearlessness embracing honesty, kindness giving space.

what I desire is who I am free with.

the only word for this is love.

HOLY WILD

my gookum said only
the wild ones are holy.

bush in northern Michigan
is the ancestral field of my body,

a girl who tastes of summer ragweed
in the high heat of noon.

my body grows by night in secret,
wet with yearling dew.

breasts and hips spread
like bushfires in a dry season,

skin pale as moonlight at dawn,
soft as a muskrat's pelt skinned in March.

my mouth is a damselfly's wings,
iridescent breath on your sex.

my hips hold a cock the colour
of crushed blueberries, bittersweet purple.

my breasts dart from your hands
like minnows, chase deeper water.

my gookum said a woman moves
like the sway of cattails in a June wind.

I lean to you like an otter dives, slick
and glistening against your chest.

underneath the cedar of my thighs,
past the birch tree of my spine

is an opening, a rattlesnake den,
when you press your body in me,

the sound I make is a blackbird's cry.
here is the wild heart of me,

rush of heat on your fullness,
this is the holy wild she made me.

a woman's sex is as sacred as her land,
my ancestors learned from creation,

a woman is as holy wild as
her body's made to be.

Boys

yes, yes,
that's what
I wanted,
I always wanted,
I always wanted,
to return
to the body
where I was born."
>   —Allen Ginsberg, "Song"

I.

the first time I realized I was wrong
was in a locker room.

I played hockey for a year,
in a room full of boys undressing,

imitating them, pretending to understand
the language of their bodies,

reading their movement
like I watched clouds in the park,

lying in a steel rocket-ship frame,
trying to trace the white bodies

of air and moisture,
looking for God in the distance between us.

one night, the men's hockey team
shared our locker room.

when the man in front of me undressed,
I felt marked by his body,

his penis as terrifying as a sudden collision
in the hallways at school,

his skin like stepping into a warm house
after walking through a frozen night,

the moment I saw what I wasn't,
interloper, alien, a ghost bird at dawn.

this is what I spent my life touching,
every time I let men fuck me,

another chance to discover what I was,
who I could and couldn't be,

when I give head, I'm charting the line
of their bodies like reading braille,

I'm searching the riverbed for rusty nails,
I'm digging a hole as deep as a grave,

I crash into them,
I ask them to make me real.

the things we want own us.

2.

I spent a summer imagining my body as different.
I grew breasts like a tomato vine grows fruit.

I rewrote my hips in fullness and fat,
my body arching up and out by night,

in daytime I hid from the sunlight,
covering this new skin under office-building shadows,

smoking in secret, denying my voice,
giving up on myself daily,

threading longing through
the smallest corridor of my eyes.

now I am as soft as boys are hard,
now I am their opposite.

when I lie naked on my bed at dawn,
I tuck my penis underneath my thighs,

erasing the last part of me that is a lie,
seeing my body as truth, unfold into sweetness.

my body bare, the inner crease of my anus
as open as a window in summer.

they can't take me anymore,
I can only be given now.

gender is a long process of offering yourself in pieces.

3.

when I was 9, a man molested me.
when I was 14, a man raped me.

my father used to whip me
with his belt after sunday sermons.

I grew salt in my veins from masculinity.

my best friend in high school
undressed before me at night,

made me hold his erect penis.
I wanted to but I didn't want to.

I wanted to be his but not as myself.
I want to rewrite my body's history,

forget the men who broke me open,
my blood between my fingers after,

teaching me to hate their bodies,
is this why I want to be a woman?

4.

the first time I saw a woman naked
I knew she was mine.

she swam in waves of light,
she was unbroken air,

she fell into an ocean of trees
and was holy.

when I look at vaginas,
I see my heart, returning to my body.

I'm tired of explaining this to men.
I'm tired of explaining this to myself.

a transsexual is a girl in the wrong body
becoming the right body in response to love.

this is the desire I have not learned to forget.

5.

is there movement between want and giving?
I have spent my life caught

between the rage of men,
the wetness of their surrender.

once I let a boy fuck me
and he holds my hand,

presses me into the mattress,
his cock inside me,

both pain and pleasure,

a sudden sharp and dull need,
he squeezes my hand as he moves,

each motion forward marked by
the tightening of his fingers on mine,

is this what men are?
the hard soft pressure in me?

I move with him in that want,
I move with his body like a boat on a lake,

each push met with surrender until we are equals.

6.

I only cum when no one is touching me.
I am free in my pleasure when men aren't watching.

I have never been allowed to be holy,
I have never been forgiven for wanting.

I have given up on their rules,
I will make my body a forest.

I will not ask them to desire me again.
I will not apologize for hope.

I masturbate imagining a man
who doesn't ask me to be quiet.

I have never been given pleasure.
I have not earned with my pain.

does this mean they have broken me
or am I unbreakable?

7.

what I want is everything
that was once mine.

the body I had before birth,
the softness I knew before bruises,

the surrender I gave
before resistance,

the moment when I can't breathe under them
and breathless, become light.

to be a girl is to know your desire
is the place you leave your lover

to walk the line of your body home
in a pleasure they feel through your breathing.

I am sometimes that girl.
I am sometimes that breath.

8.

when my body is complete,
after surgery and recovery,

after blood and breaking,
I will rewrite the history of my body.

some morning I will wake up
to not know the body I am.

I will be free, new skin, small heart,
unbroken spine bending toward clouds.

I will not be tamed or taken.
only when I love, will I be found.

I do not believe I will find
redemption or kindness.

I will carry my heart,
a newborn star,

inside my rib cage,
infinite light.

9.

for every boy who fucked me
or didn't want to fuck me,

who wondered if he could fuck me
or is ashamed to fuck me,

for calling me faggot
or seeing only a tranny,

for hurting me by being careless
or turned on by my pain,

taking more than he gives,
feeling sorry for me,

saying I wasn't sexy
because I'm shy,

for raping me
or holding my hand,

for mercy in exchange
for my strength,

to every boy I love
who sometimes loves me,

I forgive us,
I'm sorry I tried to find

my body in yours,
our desire is our difference.

you want a girl with an open cunt,
I want a boy with an open heart.

I want what
I can't have,

I give you the softness you have never given me.

10.

I have never been a boy because
I do not kill what I desire with my body.

I have always been a girl because
I resurrect myself in the night,

regrow what men take
to never give back.

this is my body,
the only one I still want,

I do not desire men,
I desire the woman I am.

I cannot forget who I used to be,
torn up, praying for him to pull out of me,

falling into empty air, looking for salvation,
receiving bruises like gifts from heaven.

I remember who I am, this girl,
she breathes in the empty room.

her breath is holy in her wanting.
her body is as bright as the moon,

I am always this girl.
I am always this breath.

Reverberation

for Wes

"This means I won't be
afraid if we're already
here"
—Ocean Vuong, "On Earth We're Briefly Gorgeous"

some nights I lean
into the shadow of our bodies,
pooling the remnant heat
the way front lawns do in summer,
alternating cycles of bask and release.

this small love is made larger
by temporality of touch,
how your hand unlocks mine
for days afterward, repeating
resonance in bone.

I like this undoing, this falling
in and breaking away, as if
we're solitary lakes meeting
against the shoreline of my legs,
your arms—we merge, let go.

the last time you held me,
your hands reached down
below my waist, cupping me
into the moment, lifting me
toward this confused softness.

am I the one who brings us
to this point of almost maybe,
or you, resting your head on mine,
tilting us to the almost possible?
I try to wash hope from my eyes.

we cross the lines we make,
my body replays yours, currents
written in the small of my back,
we're resonant, even if we fall silent,
if I leave you, if you tell me no—

some part of us breathes into air,
cherry pie, your laugh against mine,
sparks as it disappears, reverberation
is a kind of bruise. I know an echo fades.
first you fill my body like a stone.

Pretty

1.

look, you won't like this truth
every girl competes, edits herself daily

double-checks, avoids dessert.
we're born again in your eyes

        in every man's eyes

we become legendary
or not, pitiable, just friends.

a woman's face is her price tag.

2.

I know niceties demand we lie
but I'm trans, the least girl of any girl

I know how to play games
within desperation

my body marketed as experimental

save for operations to fix what can't be sold.

pretty isn't a birth trait
it's destiny.

stop reading to flip through your phone
find photos of you and who you love

weigh them

the heavier one
is your fate.

3.

I wish I could be pretty enough to matter.

even if hormones dissolve me
when surgery breaks me

I'll still be this girl, smart as a storm

sharp as a silver knife
strong as a sermon

as ugly as
she is honest.

PHOENIX

this is a trans poem. it is two poems in one body but truth lives in the centre. it does not need surgery to fix it. its preferred pronoun is a multitude. it wants to be fucked but sometimes it wants to fuck you.

I am tired of explaining the fire.

it burns because it must.

each flame is a small destiny

igniting in the heat of our bodies.

this is what you touched,

what seared us in the dark of my bedroom.

twin flames, reaching out.

your hands squeezing embers, sparking.

now we're immolated,

now we have scars that can't fade.

graft new skin to the raised edges.

I will not burn for you again.

what we brought is not what we asked for.

someday I will forgive you in a forest,

release the unanswered words.

someday you will forgive me under a mountain,

the wounded echoes.

one day we will walk over coals,

        we will call lightning,

learn to pray inside love's furnace

        without being consumed,

but I can only be this sudden torch.

        you see me now or you never will.

somewhere on your palm, a streak of me

        glimmers underneath calluses.

I brand you as holy.

few parts of me are left unchanged

        but this light remains:

wildfire, brushblaze, starburnt,

        this girl is a phoenix.

        you can't touch me without burning.

Forgiveness

1.

forgiveness is a road you walk alone
toward yourself.

at the beginning and end of the road
is the shadow of your childhood,

asleep in the fallen trees, waiting for you
to return to everything you've lost.

2.

this is the last poem I will write
about you.

I have carried you through nights
like the robin I found as a kid,

its wings broken, held from flight—
all it could be was longing for sky.

once you said you wanted lovers
to let you be yourself,

without the rules of masculinity,
to greet you like a storm

meets the city in summer,
dry heat becoming moisture,

lightning between condo towers,
momentary sound and light

breaking new ground
inside our bones.

the truth is you are the only one
who asks more from love

than what you are.
embrace yourself.

3.

. we let go in April because spring
means counting what remains.

I name you and what's gone in the hours
of sunlight returning.

this winter we built a second house
in the ruins of the first,

but I can't make you value a softness
you don't want.

still we must remember to leave an offering
for all the ghosts we made.

I am not afraid if we're already gone,
you are in me now.

our nested hearts where a chorus
of night insects swells,

your hand in mine repeats nightly,
may we always have enough

mercy for every wounded animal,
find water in every dry forest.

this what you should have learned
from my lips, explorer.

how to forgive what runs at dusk,
how to hold the threads of dawn,

to be gentle when mercy
abandons us.

4.

I have spent spring letting you go
but you return like the full moon
above the pines, distant but still
close enough to cast shadows.

I read one of your poems once—
in it, a woman says you're haunted.
her words repeated in your voice
felt like a matchstick burning down.

one of your friends tells me
it's only as bad as it feels
which means it's worse
than anyone knows.

I read a story about a woman
with a lover who rapes her
then sends an email
saying he needs space.

I cry at my desk,
embarrassed, asking—
why does this story
make me think of you?

5.

no, you get nothing more
from me than the sound

of rain through the window—
the season returns to wash

away everything we were.
forgiveness isn't knowing

why you hurt me—
it's walking home

with damp shoes,
believing the truth

lives somewhere
underground.

it reaches out,
pushes up to light

through sidewalks
and paved driveways.

when it comes,
you will be gone

but I will be here,
in a place I carry

in me like a promise.
you never held me

as if I was this truth
or this forgiveness,

but I am, I will be,
I'm already more

than you can be.
for that, only that

I forgive you
for everything.

OLYMPIA, WASHINGTON

For Dylan

I.

before our first date,
I asked if you realized
I was a trans girl, having learned
my body is sometimes a threat,
sometimes a violent desire,
never beautiful.

this was the first time
I apologized for my gender,
once after sex, I said sorry
I'm such a girl right now,
meaning sorry I'm not
enough of one.

you broke up with me
without warning, denying
my transness was why,
said you liked I was trans,
when I tell my friends, I repeat
your words like a prayer.

I realize your okcupid profile
now lists your sexuality as straight—
before me it was heteroflexible
so I cry alone in a city park.

when October comes—SRS—
my new vagina will be born
from the blood of old wounds.

2.

our second date,
I lean into you,
fold open
to folk music
while everyone
stares.

I hold your hand
under the table,
trace the skin
between us,
wild in our
convergence.

if I could,
I'd never leave
this moment,
grateful to see
love can still
touch me.

3.

how do trans girls
fall in love?

I tell my ex about you,
he says,

"that he doesn't care
you're trans

is a huge red flag—
he'll care—

by then it'll be
too late"

> *how do trans girls*
> *trust anyone?*

my friend asks if
I'm seeing anyone,

so I say I'm hanging
out with you,

she pauses then looks
down to my dick,

"is he ok with…
everything?"

> *how do trans girls*
> *have hope?*

my trans girlfriend
asks me

"do you think he broke up
with you because you

aren't feminine enough
to fall in love with?"

> *trans girls don't get answers,*
> *just questions*

from people who can't imagine
us as worthy of desire,

questions to remind us we're
not the kind of girls

boys want to
love.

4.

you kiss my neck underground,
my breasts in your hands,

my body, a river
I try to escape.

this current between us
as dangerous as anything

I've touched but you find me

inside it, move your body over me
dive into a light I don't know

I have, as if you feel
the girl I am

more than
I do.

afterwards you cradle me
press your body around mine

this is what I want, a lover
who sees me.

5.

my favourite part of us
was how we spoke
without speaking.

my hand always
caught in your hand,
divining our borders.

a casual ease
as if we had faith
in our possibility.

even in sex,
you read me
like algorithms.

instinct, intuition
I knew your mouth
in perfect detail.

this rare truth
felt like meant to be—
now I understand

it only meant
you are as wounded
as me.

6.

the last time I was with you
inside our small love, you still want me
enough to play some sad song
on your guitar in the sunroom

as your plants grow beside us.
I watch you unfold in night

momentary bloom, you are beautiful
as no other boy can ever be.

you say the plants are meditating
they reach for the distant light

so small at their roots
but then they grow green

lift up toward sunlight as if
they're sentient

in their thirst for what keeps them alive,
longing for a chance to
become whole.

same as me, a trans girl
reaching up to a faraway light I never find,

I want nothing more than what sustains me.

if you had looked at me with clear eyes,
saw my heart bend to you,

     stretching up to your face, you'd know

how precious this love was,
why I tried to hold your hand tight

     when you left me.

FUCK YOUR FEAR

I.

I can't compress this body
into language—

he asks me so I try,
argue with words,

place my tongue in the hollow of his back.

the naked boy, blond sheen in my bed, his hands

over my hips, stroke my penis
which is not a penis.

his mouth by my ear, hot air
to whisper a soft question

     "how do you get off?"

my mouth dry, I turn away.
I shrug, slight curve to my body,

I push his hands away
from my genitals,

     "I don't know but that feels male?"

gender is a small detonation
inside the space of me,

though he is steady,
adjusts his hands to follow

my back to my narrow hips,
graze my anus with his fingers

answers "ok," moves on
like it never happened—

mercy inside a war,
conscript to my body,

I fight with myself
and the language of my pleasure.

2.

I relearn masturbation after
my awkwardness with him in sex,

to hold a man's desire is
pushing my body out of my body

to give enough pleasure for him
to fall in love with the hard soft spaces

between my bones and eyes,
I will myself toward discovery—

it's easy when no one watches
to orgasm, find the emotion,

connect the feeling to the touch,
the need to the want, imagine him

over me until I hold our bodies
inside my lungs like air, then touch

myself, not as a boy would,
not as before I began,

a different pressure, pleasure
builds inside current, I'm a lake,

rock in feeling, lead to a moment
stretched out over breaths

I get off, as pain leaves me.
I don't feel shame here

even if I don't cum,
just exhale.

3.

fuck his fear like he fucked her
with his desire.

the look in his eyes, breakup
guilt merges with remorse,

a soft blue melts over him,
his hands pull his hair back,

he searches for words, locks
his eyes on hers, afraid

of what she will say,
the moisture in her eyes

as her legs shake, wait
for the moment

when he says "sorry,
but I have to go,"

her mouth forms
"fuck you,"

then his look
repeats, remorse

to guilt to fear
to hurt.

later she tells her therapist
how much she hated him then,

a boy, caught in his weakness—
her therapist asks if it's ok for him

to feel remorse about hurting her,
she says no but admits

her denial of his pain
is how she hurt him back.

4.

her mind replays the boy
she almost let fuck her,

a week after they broke up,
delirious, running south—

polish, twenty-five, and handsome,
if lost inside the complications

of his desire, how he told her
he couldn't get hard with girls

but then therapy, avoiding porn
cured him but he hasn't fucked

a girl like her, a girl inside a language
he has never put his mouth on.

she lets him trace her back,
bare skin, low-cut tank top

shows her breasts, small birds
inside their padded nests,

his eyes drop from her face
to watch her breasts move

as she breathes, his erection grows
but she slips away from him.

she is lost in other boys,
other moments, other questions

when they could or couldn't,
when they got hard or soft,

touched her breasts, her neck
then disappeared into themselves.

now it's her turn to say sorry,
pull out of his arms, her breasts

retreat to silence, unwitnessed
she closes the door behind him,

lies on her bed then goes outside to smoke,
alone in a grief she can't explain

even if anyone was willing

                      to listen.

5.

a body is a paragraph,
a poem waiting to be written.

her body is a collection
of phrases, the lips of men

eclipse her own tongue,
drown her mouth out.

        "I was curious what
        they felt like"

        translate to curious
        what she feels like

        translate to wonder
        if she's real enough

translate to image,
she is a cloud over water.

a body is a story,
a character in an imagined world.

her body is not hers,
belongs to anyone looking

to make up a new parable
of how she came to be.

"well surely your breasts
aren't real!"

translate to anger
how dare she

translate to distrust
how can she

translate to repulsion
how is she

a body is a grave,
a dead space between lovers.

her body is a burial ground
of what they left behind,

a small hope, a gentle pleasure
withers where her cunt will be.

"I've never been with
a trans before"

translate to object,
she's a foreign land

translate to experience,
she's Spain in summer

translate to experiment,
she's a disposable pleasure

a body is a promise,
a gift of histories colliding.

her body is made of moments
where grace found her,

she sleeps in forests
only she can name.

6.

please forgive him,
daughter of skies

forgive his hands
on your skin,

his cock in your mouth,
semen in your throat,

forgive how he arced
his back when cumming,

his tongue on your clit,
looking back to you

for a permission
you did not voice,

only gave with your hands
on his hair, your body

inside his body, merge
this forgiveness to love,

to regret and longing
without anger.

please forgive him,
daughter of night,

for not fucking you
when he had the chance

for his desire or undesire,
his disappearance into air

forgive his hand in your hand
everything escapes us

returns to find us holy
in our absolution.

please forgive him
daughter of daughters

to forgive yourself
for being new

remember timid
is another way to be brave

remember uncertain
is close to reverence

remember experiment
is doorway to pleasure

remember you
are not wrong

neither are your lovers
who love you—

confused and changing
like you love the earth

under the weight of spring
as summer breaks open

as everything is blessed
by its sudden wonder

forgive us our sins
daughter of yourself

as we forgive you
the miracle of your being.

7.

fuck your fear
of your body,

know it carries
the two of you

underneath dirt
inside a love

you can light
another winter with.

how he smiled
fucking you

his face over yours,
suspended together

a rapture is only
the moment everything leaves.

you are holy in
this fear, this shame

of a pleasure
still surprising.

no one sees you
without first seeing themselves.

take it back—
you are not afraid

of their discomfort
as much as you are

afraid of your unbelonging,
your wounds become honey

underneath the careful prayer
of humid winds.

say it now—
I am whole inside

the bones I carry,
fuck my fear

until it cums
rainwater.

8.

you came on my stomach
twice in twenty minutes,
less the second time.

I remember your penis
ejaculate in slow motion
as our eyes connect.

I don't cum anymore—
I borrow your moisture
to make my own wetness.

this way of fucking,
divined by you as solution
to the problem of my body

you cradle your cock
against my half-hard clit
in your right hand

flip me on my back,
fuck our genitals together
while your left arm

pushes me down hard,
grind our bodies as if
you were fucking a cis girl.

I scratch your back raw,
instinct, blind and mewing,
pressure where my vagina

will someday be makes me
orgasm in waves of sharp
electricity between bodies.

then your warm semen
pools in the cleft of me,
you hold me with hands

that smell of cock,
a not-girl, not-boy scent—
we fall asleep, confused

in our separate desire,
you, fucking me cis
me, fucked in future tense

until we break apart,
reassemble in distinct
but related universes.

later in the week
I say I like our sex
but I know we're over

when you answer back
"I'm glad to share
the experience with you."

an experience can
only happen once.
sex with me is falling

into the soft dark hole
of my body, finding comets
where other girls have cunts.

9.

poets imagine the past
as I imagine you—

the black-and-white tv set
in my gookum's attic, appear

in four channels, each one
a soft buzzing interplay

of light, dark, and specks
across the screen, aperture horizon

some nights I move the wire antennas
until the image is clear

it never lasts more than a few minutes
before losing signal, becomes

a blurred wave, your face
held over my face

your mouth on my mouth
bite my upper lip, trace

your tongue across the tip
of my nose, press into me

harder, faster, till we stutter
television raptures in b&w

us in half light,
shadow, our signals

run along our wires
until the image collapses

and the room is as silent
as it was before we came.

A Love Letter for Trans Girls

written on the one-year anniversary of my transition to the girl I was
when I started

1.

welcome to the first day of forever.

you will feel an ocean inside your chest,
a dark current of salt and plastic water bottles.

you will feel tidal waves lift and fall when you try to sleep tonight.

you will hear the slow rust song of oilers and scientific vessels.

you will feel sonar pinging off every small ache.

you will not think this is possible.
you will not think you are possible.

you are.

you are the ocean and the possible
and every body that dives deeper than we can see.

2.

you will lie to doctors.

they will ask you to describe feelings
you do not have words for.

they will make you sign a waiver
absolving them of any outcomes.

they will make you wait for months
and offer your blood to medical divination.

they will think they control your destiny
but remember, you own your body always.

you will tell them what they want to hear.
you will tell everyone what they want to hear.

you will slip past their fences and their gates.
you will climb walls,

you will steal yourself back from laboratories and therapists.
this does not make you a liar or a thief but a heroine.

3.

there will be wildfires.

friends will catch blaze and burn away.
your house will disintegrate into smoke.

the first time someone calls you a tranny on the street,
you will imagine a cavern opening up beneath you.

you will feel your skin blister from the stares of strangers.
you will live inside a constant fear that no one will understand.

you will learn to walk fast, to not make eye contact,
to listen to the same song on maximum volume with earbuds.

I recommend "Personal Jesus" but you will find your anthem.

when the fires leave, there will be a long winter.
you will taste frost every morning.

please wait for spring.

4.

death will come knocking.
he will find you between midnight and 4 am.

you will plan every moment of the next year in detail.

you will keep spreadsheets in your head
of what you can afford to change
and what you have to learn to love.

you will make suicide notes more than once.

you will know girls who kill themselves or are killed.
you will live with their ghosts, the shadows of their death,
chasing you home.

you will see icons of women burning up in their transness.
learn from their light but do not try to imitate it.

your star will not be theirs.
it will be brighter.

5.

boys will say they're curious about girls like you.
girls will dance with you at parties but never follow through.

lovers will hurt you in ways you didn't know could hurt.

boys will not fuck you
but sometimes they will only fuck you.

the balance of this is always violence.

girls will fuck you
but not introduce you to their queer friends.

the balance of this is always violence.

you will always wonder if he's fucking you because you're trans
or if she won't fuck you because you're trans.

the truth doesn't matter as much
as how it will make you doubt yourself.

remember that your lovers can embrace you
only when they learn to embrace themselves.

remember you do not carry the weight of their desire.
do not make yourself more feminine to comfort them.

do not perform your body.
be a holy place only the blessed can enter.

6.

you will learn how to walk
as if lightning trails your steps.

you will become a storm cloud in the night.
you will turn into a spring rain.

one day you will wake up and realize your body is a wild land.
you will change faster than you can name.

you will learn yourself through bad nights and mistakes.
you are a woman becoming a girl becoming a woman.

this is the most sacred celebration of the universe we know.

move between bodies in snatches of sunlight.
trace your new skin and remember you still know how to feel pleasure.

they will not take this from you.

7.

there will be a day when you will forget
how much this hurt.

you will get through laser sessions and electrolysis.

it will hurt more than anyone tells you but don't be afraid.

meditate on marsha p johnson as the machine sings.
visualize candy darling laughing in an alleyway.
channel janet mock on late-night talk shows.

you come from women who made their pain into art.
you come from women who broke open the world
so you could step into it.

let their holy flow through your eyes. you are the child of wonder.

8.

you will not see the old self in the mirror.
you will wake up and look at the girl you've always been.

the time between starting and seeing will feel infinite.
when it happens, everything will be worth it.

you will love the life you make.

even if no else loves you, even if you walk through hate,
even if they use the wrong pronoun at taco bell,

you will be ok. I promise.

9.

let me repeat this to you because no one else will.

you are loved.

the ignorance never stops hurting
but you find new things to be angry about.

you can teach them and let them into your heart
but sometimes they don't learn.

sometimes they learn from your anger,
sometimes from your mercy.

be as gentle as you can
but forgive yourself for fucking up.

you will fuck your life up so many times
you won't remember half of them.

10.

let me repeat this to you because no one else will.

you are beautiful.
you are passable.
you are desirable.
you are real.
you are a miracle and a gift.

they will try to take all of this from you every day. don't let them.

meet their shame with brilliance. welcome their dismissal with rage.
burn in every moment. be thunderous and fearless and never brave.

welcome to the first day of forever.

you are joining a sisterhood that will sometimes hold you up and
sometimes pull you down, but will always surprise you
with the depth of their power.

walk in this power.

it will feel impossible but it isn't.
this is a lie they spread to keep us from the light.

ignore them. ignore their lies and their preferred pronouns
and their identifies as a woman and their curiosity

and their erasure and their silence
and their casual violence

and just fucking ignore them.

11.

you are a promise written inside a stone.
every day, you will wash away layers
to reveal the language of your heart.

remember your lovers can embrace you
only when they learn to embrace themselves.

don't wait for them.
love yourself now.

this is the only weapon you have.

12.

let me repeat this to you because no one else will.

you are enough.

it will be the hardest thing you ever do.
it will be the best thing you ever do.

live between these truths and make a garden.
you will bloom like a wild rose.

let me repeat this to you because one else will.
you are a woman. you were always a woman.

you will become a greater woman.

someday you will believe me.
someday you won't care anymore.
someday you will be wild.

you are already whole. repeat this to yourself
if no one else will.

13.

you are the only one who is free.
your lovers will fear you for this but it is true.

the most beautiful thing about you
is not what you are but how you become.

someday you will be loved
as deeply as you want to be loved.

let me repeat this to you
because no one else will.

the most beautiful thing about you

                                        is you.

NDN Transsexual

there are no words for this hurt

      still I name myself in the colonizer's tongue
      his mouth on me, his hands on my neck

this body is a prayer he doesn't know
      to sing even when I teach him the words

once he said I only claimed to be a woman
      hear the lie inside the truth

they treat you like a woman, dirty and beat-up
      but call you a man while spitting

                choose a side
                choose a side that isn't mine

call me cedar
call me sky-blue sage
call me mashkiki[12]

      call me whore
      call me tranny
      call me white

when I transitioned, I lost my sister because
      she said I would never be a real woman

      no uterus, no children
            fake woman, pretend to be real

---

12   medicine

a woman is only her genitals in white heaven
   her sex is her worth

don't pretend it's love when it's violence
   imagine your resistance is not built

on the oppression of other bodies
   you fear

everyone leaves and the violence never ends
   try not to kill yourself before they kill you

   he texts cis girls in front of me
     tells me about his hookups

   then holds my hand, traces the hair
     out of my eyes with a shy smile

calls me his "best friend"
   gets angry when I date other boys

I'm not his and I'll never be
   I belong to secret longing

unspoken want
he kills me before
     I unmake his body with mine

   trans girl bodies are worth nothing
   unless we're dead in the papers

names on a list
   say nothing of why we die

for love and survival
for money and bad nights
for our hearts inside a gender you don't believe exists

no one chooses to be
worthless

call me wiininwaa [13]
call me zhaawandis[14]
call me wiisaakodewikwe[15]

call me missing
call me gone
call me jiibay[16]

I swallow their shame and turn it into wild light
wawatay[17] girl, piitaapan's[18] daughter

dance in the shallows of the world
burn in the ash of love

get assaulted on the street, get raped at home
get broken up with

for a white cis girl
for your genitals
for being difficult

---

13 nanabush's daughter
14 woman of the south
15 a Native woman of mixed ancestry
16 ghost
17 northern lights
18 dawn's

get chased down the street, get social media call-outs
get abused in the bedroom
get left behind

get torn apart and blamed for every sin
get likes on Instagram while he ignores you

pick a side
pick a side that isn't mine

learn to shut up
learn to disappear
forget my body, forget my sex

be punished for being thin
be shamed for this light skin

I can never be good enough

no trans woman is good enough unless
we're invisible or dead.

even when I try, I'm chasing my murder
I'm chasing my death

he will kill me someday, rape me again
no matter how sweet my skin
or soft my voice

keep trying, try harder, try more
make myself real

surgery is the only

way out.

pain will not save me
     nor fame nor success nor intelligence nor beauty nor grace
     nor mercy nor faith nor culture nor wisdom nor strength nor compassion

     nor any white man's love.

some girls are made to be murdered
     and I'm one of them

call me wiingashk[19]
call me semaa[20]
call me zoongide'ewin[21]

     kill me
     kill me
     kill me

my blood is your redemption

     the first thing the Spanish did when they got here
was throw all the indigenous trans women into a pit
     of starving dogs to be torn apart and eaten

you haven't stopped doing it since
     got us bleeding and naked and dead
between your legs.

sometimes I pray

19   cedar
20   tobacco
21   courage

but it never helps

be offended by this poem
 be offended by this gender

   this anishinaabemowin this poor translation
   this cunt made from a cock
   this surgical body this vulgar revelation
   this transsexual heart this NDN mind
this humanity this claim to existence
   this refusal to die to go away to shut up

fuck you and your gods
 terra nullius of the body
   fuck you and your good NDNs
 dance for them if you want to but
   I won't perform apology

fuck this body as it breaks in his hands

 he loved me, you know
 he loved me, just not enough

I let him use me until there is nothing left to use
 it's the best love I have
 it's the only love I can get

you made a country out of me
 you made a nation in me

 and I'm the one
 who isn't real?

have your kingdom
      your holy land

I will not walk there
      among the cis and blessed

          because

the only sacred thing about me
      is how I survive you.

Niibii

for wes

I.

anishinaabe women speak for the water
        in lodges filled by smoke and night

when I was young, I learned from old women
        how we sing for our lakes

pray to mishomiisinaak with copper cups
        of niibii, ode'min[22] in bowls

our bodies, offerings and vessels
        to the unknowable gizhe-manidoo[23].

2.

our first flirtation, you send me a photo
of a lake in Minnesota,

fulfill my request to you:
        take pictures of lakes,

my precognition of our love,
your anthropological study of waterways

mirrors your anthropological study
of the female body, this anishinaabe body

---

22   strawberries
23   creator

runs through your fingers, leaves you
damp with jiibaa, ghosts of me

        drown in your blue eyes,
swim in your Instagram.

we break up for the first time,
then meet for coffee three months later

I say we are like separate lakes, overgrown
        you reply "maybe we meet at our edges"

but our edges are not the soft spill
        of waterways colluding into breath,

just another story of a white boy
        leaping into wet skyline, leaving

muddy footprints along my spine,
        our ancestral history repeats:

you conquer me, catch and release
        without ever learning

my name.

3.

niibii is sacred like the anishinaabe women
we hold it in our bodies,

menstruation is water returning
to the centre of the universe,

too powerful, miskwi mashkiki,[24]
for ceremony,

anishinaabe women bleed
                on lake islands into moss

while creation opens
                around them.

no one does this anymore
                        but we still remember.

anishinaabe niizh ode kwe[25]

        don't say I claim to be a woman
        don't say I assert the identity of a woman

niizh ode kwe care for other kwewak
        on moontime, medicine is

just listening to akii
close like niibii does.

it's all gone now, my shoreline
evaporated into cottages.

they took it away, filled us with poison
        and zebra mussels, Asian carp.

there's mercury in my akiiton[26]
and ore tailings in my liver.

---

24   blood medicine
25   two heart woman
26   vagina

white cis girls take photos
        by our lakes and filter them

into sepia light, intersperse
        their bodies around

dead Indian bones and holy zaaga'igan[27]
        and we are not allowed to complain

but sometimes I still do, never learning
        an Indian woman's place is shut up

in an alleyway, dumped down
        a hotel laundry chute.

niibii listens, niibii knows where we go
when we disappear

        inside a lake is niibii's heart
        she grows back

like a good NDN woman does,
        gets larger despite their thirst

blooms by rainfall, returns
        to us in the arms of spring,

laughs with one hand over her face
        looks away, embarrassed

---

27 lakes

she is nimama miinwa inawemaagan[28]
aasha biidwewebiisaa[29]

she comes back as all anishinaabe women do
to the waters that birth us.

4.

you said you would take me swimming
            in Lake Ontario but you took

cis girls instead, disappear us
            into absence as if I were a bad night

      you want to forget, as if intimacy
was another word for exploration

I'd been mapped out by you in secret,
            lies and half truths and they never knew

about me, not the truth of me and you
            our bodies mixing under currents,

your hand on my throat as you press
            into me like ice floes descend

to fill the inlet northern bay,
            cold everywhere as your eyes

flinted against mine, my breasts
            soft under you until you cum

---

28   my relation
29   I hear the rain start

inside me, pull out and leave,
        a fluid erasure of time.

once you took your ex-girlfriend
        on a camping trip to Lake Superior

posted a photo of her with the caption
        gichigami, the anishinaabe name

I taught you, rearticulating me
        back to a colonial audience

performing wokeness in pedagogy,
        speaking about temporality

and intimacy and collusion and rupture
        and embedded research and Spain

chasing waterways everywhere you go,
        brown women, black women, Indian women

new worlds to drink and pour out
        into research, soak your body

in our orgasms until you shine
        with our waters, redeemed.

your ancestors came here on ships
        searching for home and I let you

steal mine without saying anything,
        I always knew you would never

swim with me in a lake,
       I'd drown you with the wonder

of a woman in waters
       you can never claim.

5.

niibii is ceremony,
soaked in cedar or poured

on mishomisanaak in a lodge
       of bent willow branches.

once I knew an anishinaabe woman
       and all she did was travel

over Ontario doing cedar bath ceremonies
       for anishinaabe women who'd been raped

or beaten by men, she told me
healing was in niibii, our first mother

along with akii, the one who never
       leaves us, even when we die.

this ceremony, she said, is just
       reminding these women

that they are loved and it's ok
       to sometimes be broken,

even if you are alone, her hands dip into water,
she says you have niibii inside you,

remember that, she nods to me,
remember you carry your mother

    always.

6.

I can't heal from you
    but I try

to draw you out of my skin
    in lodges, with elders

across the country, smudging
with sweetgrass because it makes

your spirit soft in new growth,
    offers beginnings.

you were the first boy
    to touch my breasts,

the first boy to feel
    my new hips,

the first boy who watched
    my body change over

from oak to willow, gripped
    my hand in yours as tight

as anyone has ever held me
          then said I wasn't real,

asked me if you fucking me
          was how I validated myself

as a woman, said a thousand things
that tore me open, push pull

love affair while you chased
          cis women and men,

complained to me about your lovers,
          asked for my care, holding you

in the dark, trans girl shame
          grows in me like Queen Anne's lace.

then rupture, disappearing from me
          and pretending not to see me

in public but never leaving,
          still you send me messages

saying you love me but won't
          face up to that love.

I've prayed and prayed
          to ancestors

during sleepless nights after texts
          from you accusing me of some mistake,

how you claimed that our intimacy
        was coerced, that I pressured

you into touching me or provoked
        you into saying transphobic shit,

repeating their lies again, white men
        afraid of Indian whores, transsexual predators.

my aunties tell me to walk away,
        my sisters cursed you,

but I still hold you in me
        like a stone in my heart,

you are your mother, a distance
        that can't be crossed, a refusal

to love, you are your father,
        conquering foreign bodies

without accountability to harm,
        and I am my gookum's daughter,

bruises around my eyes, thinking
        I could heal you if

I was just sweeter, softer
        if I tried harder to love you,

you stop hurting me, but that's
        what it means to a native woman

400 years after genocide began here,
        telling yourself it's your fault

the world is broke open,
        dressing in their clothes,

lying in their beds, taking it
        to give new life

to countries you will never
        be safe in.

you are your ancestors
        and I am mine,

the water between us as wide
        and furious as the St Lawrence,

when you leave for Spain,
        I'll be sad and happy

finally free of you but never
        at peace with what

you did while you were
        here.

7.

niibii is endless

        despite pollution
        despite oil pipeline

despite border disputes
despite trade agreements
despite incursions
despite hydro dams
despite mercury
despite whiteness
despite dead NDN bodies
despite you.

niibii was first

before the land
before the sky
before the light
before the thunders
before anishinaabe
before all beings

she was an entire universe
and she will be one again.

muskrat dove to her bottom,
brought up soil, made land

and she nurtured forests into worlds,
gave life from her blood.

niibii can be hurt
but she can't be murdered

her daughters can be hurt
be murdered

but like her, we are

       the first
       the infinite
       the new
       the life
       the beginning
       the wonder
       the beauty
       the blessed

we return, niibii returns
       we heal, niibii heals

    in eight weeks I'll have surgery
a vagina in waves of blood and pain,

alone in a hospital room in Montreal
      you won't be there, even though

you said you would be, texted me
      to say I should let you know

if I'm ok after the surgery,
      ignoring I'm scared, ignoring you pushed me

to get this surgery, the only way
       you'd ever see me as real

then letting me know you still won't
      think I'm a woman

     even after but still

you want to know that I'm ok?

well I'm not ok, babe
        kisaakihin[30]

but niibii has me,
        niibii and all my ancestors

my grandmothers inside my marrow
        sing in their lodges.

I was born to pain
        but also water

and it runs through me
        even as you leave me.

8.

niibii is a river
        running past borders

niibii is a trans girl
        broken open

still moving toward
        home, her beginnings

in estuaries, in snow melts
        her name is kiiwe[31]

---

30 I love you
31 goes home

ani-giiwen, nidaanis
you abused me

like every woman you take
and throw away,

disposability is a queer politic
anthropology is another word

for rape, me crying
in the bathroom

after you use me
like you use water

to wash my blood off
your cock.

but rivers and trans girls know something
you will never know

how to find our way back
across wastelands

to the lakes we belong to,
kiiwe is a verb but also a promise.

Tonight

tonight I'm tired of being your ghost
     a small nothing you pour your body into

    tonight I hold you
        in my throat like birth

    tonight I breathe with you
        rest my cheek on yours

                then let you go
                to the other girl waiting.

    place your hand
        between my legs

    force your mouth
        down to my breasts

    let you lift me by my hips
        throw me against the wall

    I fall apart beneath you
        you fuck me

           incoherent and crying

    tonight I'm as ready to live
            as I am to die.

after we cum
      I ask you
                  if you know how hide becomes soft
                      as you check your phone
                        to text her back

I say
      first you cut the skin from the animal
          blood against blade

reveal the bones
the wild muscle

          the ruptured heart.

then dry and wash
      the brain crushed into the skin

      leave to soak
hang in the afternoon sun

      rinse repeat
        until

the new body emerges
            from the broken open

      the animal dies
        but isn't gone

becomes as soft
      as it was hard

you don't understand a word of this.

but I let you trace my lips
  with your fingers

       I bite them
         and smile

I close my eyes when you

      kiss me

        goodbye.

  I walk home
    as you go to fuck her

      you text me at 4 am

       "I love you"
     and
       "I'm sorry I hurt you."

       your love repeats
       my history.

your ancestors saw the infinite of this land
     named it fear and tried
       to kill it
   you saw me
     and didn't know if you should
    love me or
       run from me

tonight I let you do both
        but I won't be the cis girl
          in your bed

      I didn't come here
        to sing your wounded body whole

      though evergreens bloom between my legs
         and tobacco leaves grow inside my heart.

tonight
        I will be more
           than the dead trans girl on the news

        more than the noble NDNs
          in your land acknowledgement.

tonight
    you will conquer me
      and I will not disappear

        this is how I know

             I'm holy

tonight
      my body is not terra nullius
        and you won't save me

     I am the wild
       that is not empty

          the animal
           that is not dead

and the girl
  you won't call yours

but this is not a prayer
  and we are not sinners
    to be redeemed

I will not call you wrong
  to be afraid to love me

        in your bed at daylight

even if bruises on my thighs
  flower from your mouth

          by dawn.

I am not a confession
  you make in secret

not a servant of God to rest my hands
  on your face and forgive you

      for sins I don't believe in.

I am not Eve's daughter
  but Ayaash returned
    to Akii

I will not explain what these words mean
  even if I love you
    more than I love myself

I will text you back
a heart emoji

because tonight
I am not the ghost you leave behind
but a softness

you will never know
how to be.

Acknowledgements

I am grateful to Canisia Lubrin for her editorial support, friendship, and tremendous poetic intelligence, as well as Jay and Hazel Millar for their support in the writing of this book.

I am thankful for those I love and who love me. To Wesley Brunson—for better and often worse, I found myself through loving you.

For this painful and joyous life, I am always grateful.

GWEN BENAWAY is a trans girl of Anishinaabe and Métis descent. She has published two collections of poetry, *Ceremonies for the Dead, Passage, Holy Wild* and her fourth collection, *Aperture*, is forthcoming from Book*hug in Spring 2020. Her writing has been published in many national publications, including CBC Arts, *Maclean's Magazine*, and the *Globe and Mail*. She is currently editing an anthology of Fantasy short stories by trans girl writers, *Maiden Mother Crone*, and working on a book of creative non-fiction, *trans girl in love*. She lives in Toronto, Ontario and is a Ph.D student at the Women and Gender Studies Institute at the University of Toronto.

Manufactured as the First Edition of
Holy Wild in the Fall of 2018
by Book*hug.

Distributed in Canada by the Literary Press Group:
www.lpg.ca

Distributed in the US by Small Press Distribution:
www.spdbooks.org

Shop online at www.bookthug.ca

BOOK
PRODUCTION
WAR ECONOMY
STANDARD

Edited for the press by Canisia Lubrin
Copy edited by Stuart Ross
Type + design by Kate Hargreaves